Please Do Not Feed the Ghost

Peter Ramos

BlazeVOX [books]

Buffalo, New York

Please Do Not Feed the Ghost by Peter Ramos
Copyright © 2008

Published by BlazeVOX [books]

All rights reserved. No part of this book may be reproduced without
the publisher's written permission, except for brief quotations in reviews.

Printed in the United States of America

Book design by Geoffrey Gatza
Cover: video still from *Living Pictures* (Laundromat), 2003, by Monica Duncan
and Lara Odell

First Edition

ISBN: 1-934289-55-8   ISBN 13: 978-1-934289-55-6
Library of Congress Control Number : 2008920494

BlazeVOX [books]
14 Tremaine Ave
Kenmore, NY 14217
Editor@blazevox.org

publisher of weird little books

BlazeVOX [books]

blazevox.org

2   4   6   8   0   9   7   5   3

Acknowledgments

Grateful acknowledgment is given to the following journals and anthologies where versions of these poems have appeared or are forthcoming:

"Before They Found Mrs. McFarland in Her Car," *Acorn Whistle*
"Rotten May Pole," "History," and "Crossing Minnesota
    at Night," *Artvoice*
"Mid-Century Modern" and "The Drunk," *Black Bear Review*
"Me and Old Robert McGee," *Black River Review*
"Pan American," *Card Catalogue Poetry Project*, Ed.
    Lisa Forrest (Buffalo: One Eared Rabbit Press, 2004)
"The Put-Together Wedding Cake" and "Out-Patient Walk-In,"
    The Chattahoochee Review
"The Nineteenth Century," *Fugue*
"The Beautiful Aunt," *The Gihon River Review*
"Birthday," *Indiana Review*
"Birthday," "The Put-Together Wedding Cake," "The Nineteenth
    Century," "John Berryman in my Dreams" and "Fathers
    and Sons," *Junta: an Anthology of Avant-Garde Latino/a
    Writing*. Ed. Gabriel Gomez (Santa Fe)
"On Majoring in English," *Kiosk*
"Summer," *Maverick* (online)
"Evolution," *Meridian*
"John Berryman in my Dreams" and "Fathers and Sons,"
    MIPOesias (online)
"Letter to Tu Fu," *Ocho*
Section 12. of "Watching Late-Night Hitchcock," *Painted
    Bride Quarterly*
"Telemachus," "Año Nuevo, 1992" and "Lush Life," *Poet Lore*
"Polaroid," "Crystal Meth" and "Immigrant," *Rio Grande Review*
"Short Waves," *Slipstream*
"Midnight in the Sapphire Lounge" and "Employment in
    Kaplan's Brass Shop," *Square One*
"Please Do Not Feed the Ghost," "Pink," "Pornography," and
    "Iphigeneia," *Verse*

Grateful acknowledgment is also given to Frank E. Smith for publishing some of these poems in a White Eagle Coffee Store Press chapbook, and to Kristen Gallagher for publishing "Watching Late-Night Hitchcock" and several of these poems in a Handwritten Press chapbook. I would like to thank the Constance Saltontsall Foundation for the Arts for providing me the time and space to work on many of these poems.

Contents

John Berryman in my Dreams 11

The Put-Together Wedding Cake 12

Birthday 13

Summer 14

Año Nuevo, 1992 15

Polaroid 16

Mid-Century Modern 17

History 18

Pink 19

Pornography 20

The Drunk 21

Please Do Not Feed the Ghost 22

The Nineteenth Century 23

Out-Patient Walk-In 24

Telemachus 25

Short Waves 26

Watching Late-Night Hitchcock 27

Fathers and Sons 47

Age of Reason 48

Evolution 49

Employment in Kaplan's Brass Shop 50

On Majoring in English 51

Midnight in the Sapphire Lounge 52

Crystal Meth 53

Rotten May Pole 54

Iphigeneia 55

Before They Found Mrs. McFarland in Her Car 56
The Beautiful Aunt 57
The Man who Sold the World 58
Me and Old Robert McGee 59
Southern Gothic (Abridged) 60
Letter to Tu Fu 61
Lush Life 62
Pan American 63
Crossing Minnesota at Night 64
Waiting for the Firstborn 65
Immigrant 67

Notes 69
Biographical Note 71

B   *X*

Please Do Not Feed
the Ghost

John Berryman in my Dreams

Blacking out in some basement café, crowded
And alone in the sad mid century, I come back & go on
Hunting powder-puff angels, the pan-caked faces

Under bangs cut straight, the puckered mouths wet
With lipstick. Then do I move through night, glass
After each empty glass—am I all right?

Sure be: Henry's famous, even hip.
The kids pick me out in the dimmest bars
Or slopping late in the Chinese joints

Of Boston, on the make. It's always time
To get stuffed. Here's the edge of awake—
Cocktails, pack of matches, somebody's face

Watery-familiar. Hi there, stranger.
Here's to being up for something beautiful,
Regrettable and sore.

The Put-Together Wedding Cake

They've gone to a cocktail party,
gone to Hawaii for pot roast.
Find it on the coffee table, the cake

that is, that is real but glowing
in a living room milder than Heaven.
You've never seen a cake like this—
blue bamboo on icing smooth as wallpaper.
But you must join the pinker

to the darker figurine, plastic hand
in plastic hand. How will you speak for them?
The groom is learning the language, dull-eyed
for remembering what they said: "America the gold
and golden fleece!" The bride thinks of daffodils
which turn into kitchen gloves.

Hers is not gold but white
as an icebox.

Birthday

A little after midnight—the skies clear
over Washington D.C., below freezing
at Dulles International Airport,

the sloping lines of its buildings
disappear into the snow, the plowed snow
spilling over the walkways thick

and powdery as cake-mix. Lit by floodlights,
baggage handlers push the stacked luggage
between sliding glass, follow the well-dressed

as jet engines whine. West of the continent,
eight thousand miles across the Pacific,
a small jungle village explodes—

This is your home. This frosty distance
under the moon. In secret locations, the astronauts—
declassified—slip into their bright suits.

Summer

watching loudmouth noon

                                            from the toolshed

from the fire road or the graveyard

                                            end of July   short cut

hush the green wheat

                                            barn I'm afraid of

come to tag the tree

                                            the others burst all directions

fireflies   my bedtime

                                            mooney face tell me

a story

                                            window swallow me

Año Nuevo, 1992

The men cough and snort
over cards as palm trees rattle

down the afternoon. By night,
they say, the president cannot tell

the mountains from night.
Or its many dwellers. The hour

arriving, the frogs alert the moon
beneath torn banana leaves.

And grandmothers whisper at the table
in light the color of rum or sweat

through midnight
under the chipped Jesus.

Even the children lean
out of the searchlights, their cigarettes

puncture the darkness.
Once drunken sequins rang

like Bolívares on the bellies.
But the soldiers ungather.

They empty their clips
into the stars.

Polaroid

Uncle Jack—
a month before the accident, standing
in his bedroom slippers by the green carport
in late April. He'd been married a year

in which he perfected his swing,
poured himself highballs
and busted his thumb
while plumbing. *So there*

he'd say and says it here
with his grinning mug—just behind him
the great magnolia, his last, blooming
white as a Cadillac,
red as a Miami burn, pink
as a pin-up's nipples.

Mid-Century Modern

They rust now in the innards,
in the plumbing's guts. Under linoleum,
secret in dry-wall, torn paper, they
bloom beneath layers of paint.
They are jewels in pitch glue,
asleep in the bracebeams.

Their basement freezer gurgles
all night, the crudded screen doors
bang and bang.

Bluing the bedrooms,
the leafloam in window-wells,
they touch the porcelain,
gray aluminum,
the heating ducts and water pipes
with a quaint, inscrutable faith:

O toasters and cut-sandwich trays!
O State-of-the-Art Norge,
Sunbeam, General Electric!
O voltage, long past
their darkness, still crackling.

History

By the X-ing light
covered with rust, what's left

of the brakeman-shack
lingers a moment,

weathered, worn down to dull
silver paper on which —*lick me*

or *Todd + Becky Forever*—children
take their turns

defacing the page, making it
more itself than ever.

Pink

Fingernails click the glass
bar-top. Grenadine

bleeds a cocktail.
You put on lipstick and drug

your elegant grandmother:
it's Happy Hour, the big comeback,

your turn to shiver
in sequins like a star.

Pornography

The hornet crawls in
through the open window.

I'm always home. All day
it skitters and knocks

beneath a bright ceiling
until the fountain stops

falling or I quit
trying to word it.

The Drunk

I open my door and he's there, winking—
shadowy thin, he slips in like a dime.
We glide all night, open to strangers.
He sings to me of nymphs, of bellies
and lips and lashes. "I know them all," he tells me,
slapping my back. I am filled and full
of his bravado. The world is small enough to eat.
The spring is budding into night.
"Just look at that hair," he says,
"taste the shapes with your eyes."

And I do—until I'm all nerves,
warm flesh and blood. Until I weep
for haunches and laugh at the trees.
I slump in his arms and he carries me home.
He opens my door and undresses me.
I giggle in the dark as he dumps me in bed.
Now he pulls down the covers
while soothing my brow. I say,
"You are beautiful. You are my father."
He says, "you are anything you want." Now

I remember how it goes.
I close my teeth and clench my eyes.
He puts his mouth to my ear,
cocks his fist and, whispering filth,
pounds my body toward dawn.

Please Do Not Feed the Ghost

October, color gone from the wheat
and you straggle back, howling
in your pulled wool, your work boots,
come to yuck it up with me, your mouth
full of loam, jacket lined with rot, crazy
as the leaves.

Each time I try to sleep you off, hoping winter
will stamp its feet, sober you up.
But the hallways soften. You
stuff me full of mothballs.

The Nineteenth Century

There was nothing left on earth
to discover, so we finally took sick.

Low doses of mercury prescribed
by the physicians kept us in bed

long afternoons, the curtains blowing
through open windows and at night

we dreamt of children—their milky limbs
and torsos androgynous. Convalescing,

we spoke of our lives, gatherings
at Harper's Ferry, speculations out West,

the words we left in our boot-prints: *Turkey Foot,
Indian Grass, Rattlesnake Master*.

History groaned, the millennium approached—
we knew this but succumbed in the end

to fits of nostalgia, to bourbon and verses
of Jimmy Crack Corn until dawn.

And yet—to have gone out
the other way—beside the river—

bright-eyed and shirtless, exsanguinating,
our teeth exposed in the dim daguerreotypes…

Out-Patient Walk-In

When Lilly with her one remaining hand
opens the door, the city leaps in, a lion: a burst
of traffic, bricks and broken light that holds.
But the room comes back aspirin white. The muzak drops
its petals. And Lilly is crying, crossing herself
at the metal detector. She clutches her bag of candy,
shaking with medication. Everyone manages not to stare,
even the paramedic, wheeling a stretcher
past her now with walkie-talkie and swagger,
handsomely bored. He knows Lilly, gives her
the back of his skull. And she knows him
as she begins to lift now and swell with something
defiant, like love itself, calling out "Jesus
loves you, hon. You're one of the superstars!"

Telemachus

An emerald ghost, the ocean
rubs and punishes this island, this bony coast,
tosses turns the boat that keeps me near
in my bright straw hat and swimming trunks become
too small. The sky darkens, churning blue cream.

By the dock the wind stiffens
my mother's pale skin. In soaked white cotton,
under straw hut, she sips Pepsi Cola
from a straw, barefoot, and smiles on me—my mother
around whom the vegetation riots.

Six months ago, on a two day drunk, father slumped
out of midnight mass, the wet night lit by firecrackers.
He flashed and disappeared. Palm trees clattered,
stirred my dizzying blood. In my father's country
everything grows.

Short Waves

Lonely son of a drinker, my father slept
uneasily, his throat swollen with a delicate creature—
something tiny that cried and fluttered to life one morning
in Caracas, after his father had come home late.
The old man had forced the bedroom door.
He'd stroked the child's face, parted my father's lips
to reach into that dark space
just under the voice.

Imagine the stirring, the soft violence
in the neck when my father awoke
hearing that awkward song blossom. How could he
know his own voice, waiting as he did
to cross water, to live in a new land, hoping
the words would fit in his mouth?

He learned, somehow.
He grew into his suit, kept his mouth shut
with cigars. At night he switched on
the short wave—salsa from his country blaring,
wheezing with static, drowning him out
as he coughed up feathers.

In a photograph
my father waves a white handkerchief,
the eyes ghosted by flashglare,
mouth open, a lopsided O of worn teeth.
Inside, the unkillable bird works quietly,
so at home by now. Glazed and drunk,
his face wrung out at last, my father strains.
He almost sings.

Watching Late-Night Hitchcock
—24 Frames

1.
What you *can*not regulate—animals
or wayward love, the man in brushed black,
in tails and hat, immaculate

but for his left boot polished *erotic*
on which has fallen a droplet still fresh
and bright crimson—is difference, *desire,*

the aristocracy you wanted
and shrank before, certain fate,
an insistence on blood.

2.
As in dreams, the predominant
        though complicated theme is touching
        what's otherwise forbidden:

coconut cake, the chesty peroxide-
        blonde, a kitchen knife.
        The living room is dark

except where the black and white movie
        flickers light on the wall.
        My great-grandmother lived here

alone to keep the place gleaming. Did she
        scour each crevice? Her obsessions press.
        The wainscoting needs dusting.

3.
Nana, you swore off Newport
when the festivals began, when the jazz
and large packs of "riffraff"

showed up. In Hollywood's heyday
you turned thirty and drove all the way back
from Reno divorced.

4.
The dapper lead takes a sip
and says nothing, he thinks
They're all dye-jobs, you know it
and I know it. Ten to one
Blondie's not real under that skirt.

5.
Hard candy, car keys
and tranquilizers all mixed up
in a cobalt finger bowl:

she turned off the Hi-Fi
then put on her white gloves—your daughter,
grown up & out of the house.

6.
Then it was summer, blue-blooming
hydrangeas, Naval uniforms
and crossed anchors embroidered.
It was Lowell and Winthrop,

Dickinson, even the Kennedys
and never you. It was a Lady
—no relation—blue veined
and bathing in the cold Atlantic.

7.
Then another war, followed by bulldozers
and house after duplicate house, each one
radiant, sustained by the airwaves,

by cooling units in a dry month
and buckets of ice cream in the white freezer.
The lawn sprinklers thudded

illegally in the dark.
But the weather wouldn't last. They joked
and put out a small pitcher of martinis to soak.

8.
The suburbs, that's what
my father wanted—if possible,

to marry into them. My mother?
A clean and bright kitchen

where you never have to touch
what you eat. I wanted cake—the pink

and white delectable

9.
Dear Mother:

I can still hear the bright name—
Miami—and see us arriving

late at night in the lobby,
wondering past the plastic banana plants,

the old men in wet lemon
guayaberas. I knew

you'd refuse the room
they offered us—all those torn dirty pictures

on the floor! And the dark blue carpet you said
was wet with God-knows-what. We left

to eat dinner that night in a "greasy-spoon."
Such new words flew out of you

when Dad lifted me up and held me
over the balcony. The aqua-bright

swimming pool rose up
and panted the building green.

Thanks for the vacation, Mother,
now that we're home you can finally quit—

Mush love,

10.
        Trajection

of gas and highways

                to the starter homes

of ceiling fans to the dropped

                ceilings to the long

rockets to the glinting

                tinsel-bright satellites beyond

now it's late a settling

                down by the liquor store

alarm-tape lining the plate-glass

                windows vacancy

in the last motel:

          11.
        fishnets
   and garter-belts

            the nurse's uniform
     or other get-ups in rubber
the ugly horse-painting

    this movie
              that one

12.
And before we know it, the sexy lead is
—Mother of God!—rubbed out.

It turns out we don't know exactly
what we want. Rilke wrote that beauty is nothing

but the beginning of terror. That's fine
for Germany, Prague or wherever. Not here.

We like things clean: the boat flag
snapping in the breeze,

the platinum bee hive
sipping gin from a bird bath.

13.
I slip
into your daughter's blue,
embroidered

make up
yr. mind
you Tiresias
if you know
know damn well
or else
you don't

Japanese housecoat
brought back
from the war

14.
How you bristled
when the neighbors called you "blue blood."

I'm a grocer's daughter, you snapped
but swelled when your second husband,

"The Skipper," a Commodore,
got your name in the

Social Register—Mable Norton Fenn—
or when the guard stiffened

and saluted the star on your windshield
at the Newport Navy Base or the Boston Yard.

Trapped at ninety
in your stroke-frozen frame, you spoke your last

to the live-in nurse: *Hurry up, Louise,
bring my make up and brush!*

15.
Uncle Buddy,
your openly bigoted brother
always mixed up you'd say

in the wrong crowd
bought himself a motor lodge in North Jersey,
                adding the lounge

later   one night in '42 (Halloween)
Cab Calloway shows up practically made

of money, drunk and eloquent
each word a sparkling hundred grand

and it went — so they say — like this:

Got a match, mac?

                    —*It's 'Buddy'*

Now don't get sore, man —
                —*Listen up you greasy pimp, you*
      take your lousy houndstooth jacket and scram!

And lit his own cigar, *Drinks on the house!*
grinning

              until he found the note

    his lovely wife left him.

16.
Let's get you a cocktail dress,

                              you said. *You never know*

just when you'll need it.

17.
Once again I'm seven, awake and aware
      I've wet your bed, soaked through

the white sheets to the whiter, pilled bedspread.
      Soon Mother will enter the room, letting the light in

the harsh bright New England light of old—
      Knock! Knock!

18.
Drum the tom-tom
Snip the hi-hat
Strum the catgut

Finger-pluck the bass note
the blue note

flutter-beat THUMP

BASS DRUM

The Rumba
The Samba
The Foxtrot   *Go!*

Bongo Jazz
Cha-Cha-Cha!

Put on your lipstick honey
we're all out of ice

19.
Buddy's — OP N LATE

swizzle sticks in the dim

        a blue jukebox

institutionalized boozing

        going dry, going

belly up twenty years

        after the War. Thirty.

The cheap-drink hour

        extends

20.
Diamond Anniversary

Through silver pleated drapes they take in
each winter the deep iridescent snow, the drifts
blown smooth as cake-frosting.

They drink a little, survived wars,
the Great Society and bubble lights
on a white Christmas tree.

At night, in their separate beds, they swallow
pink sedatives, behold the moon
through cold panes of glass.

21.
    (Knock! Knock!)

Noon. Glass of milk, a turkey sandwich —
cut across end to end, the crumbs
lit by sunlight on Bone China.
Piano at three. A vase of Blue Delphinium

for Mother under the staircase.
Dust the light fixtures and candelabra.
Comet the bathrooms.
Polish the brass fruit.

22.
Pluck the catgut!
Without your dull leather gloves,
with fingers and thumb

pluck the catgut!
The house is drizzling, empty
and cold, the fuses long blown.

There is no moon.
What's living or buried
in the basement can wait.

So pluck the catgut!
Pluck! Pluck!
Pluck the catgut!

23.
Beneath my skinned knee
and all around me stretched
that wide carpet, neat-napped and smart
Puritanical gray, with several straight-backed chairs,
the seat cushions hand-stitched
in Boston, and placed
on a pea-green shelf, just out of my reach,
                      a white box
of ribbon candy

shining in the window light.

        *   *   *

Once, your Japanese woodcut
framed in Newport
fell clattering to the hardwood floor.
And I came running

to you—Nana.
Nothing could keep me
from your dark Victorian bed,
from fingering the headboard's
carved angels and grapes.

24.
You're not starving, *dear.*
People in Ethiopia starve, but you

are merely hungry. And please
don't shout. Tragedies happen,

it's true, but luckily enough
infrequently. I told your mother the same

and she was lovely
to me, so kind in the otherwise

uneventful end. Now,
What I wouldn't give

to witness a turquoise sky,
even from some dingy cafeteria booth.

And you could do worse than take my love
for clean forms, what you call

my 'bone-white austerity.' You, dear,
might do with my endurance and pluck.

You could certainly afford a touch
more temperance in the blood.

Fathers and Sons

I slam my bedroom door, drop the needle on Led Zeppelin III
and turn the volume knob all the way. *That'll show him.*
But my father's gone: already traveling back to Venezuela,
back to his childhood home, to the old bedroom. Arriving,
he finds the radio still there, dusty glass tubes glowing
in its back. He slams his own bedroom door and tunes
until he gets an American station—Motown, The Four Tops.
A ha!, he says, *Toma esto!* But his father, dead and buried,
now begins knocking as loudly as possible the right side
of the wooden coffin, a tango rhythm he remembers perfectly,
insistent, bright—and so on toward the beginning.

Music guides the patriarchal line of my family, to music
we stage our frustrated coups. What else can we do?
We are not kings.

Age of Reason

At fifteen his heart's a transistor
under red maples picking up books
voices, chords and landscape

the afternoon's
blue beyond which
throb satellites.

Evolution

I.

      I am seven and two
      monkeys are doing it right
      and right before me, the one—
      to which is attached a kind of black
      Q-tip—giving it to the other.

II.

      As it happens,
      my Uncle Gene clears the large crowd
      from the monkey house. He has just explained
      for my benefit
      the whole routine out loud.

III.

      I turn sixteen
      and lose my virginity.
      Some theories are useless
      as our meddling relatives.
      Go fuck yourself, Uncle Gene.

Employment in Kaplan's Brass Shop

I didn't notice until later, long after that summer
when I'd stick a Spackle-knife in my back pocket,
swing an aluminum ladder toward the high ceiling, then climb up
and up with my brushes, bucket of thinner and tin can of latex
to stroke on coat after coat of vermilion.

From morning to dusk, when the light tubes clicked on
in Kaplan's Antiques Brass Shop, I'd hang there,
ten feet above all that junk—the clocks and weather vanes,
brass fish and candelabra—while the girl with red hair
worked the register or stared out, her chin soft

as a plum in her palm. For two months
I rubbed a band of paint around the store while below
she re-arranged the counter and never looked up. I know
she hated that job, but when she'd sing to herself
out of witless boredom, the whole place dead by three…

She finally left, of course, and I came down
to polish the brass beds, working up that luster until it shone
bright as a trumpet's and the shop rang
with brilliance, my small praise to the mother—
unreachable—who beats us while we sing.

On Majoring in English

That summer after graduation, play it real clean.
Read *Moby Dick* in your parents' basement
or something. Wait til August, then spend the night
in a beach house with your brother and two women
you meet on the boardwalk. Leave your body somehow
in the sunroom, rain drumming out the skylights.
Burn cork and smear the ashes on your face.
Chase the women around the room, weeping and waving
an iron ladle. They might later say how enormous
your eyeballs looked.

Midnight in the Sapphire Lounge

There is someone else,
some blind elastic blue body in mine,
his eyes coal zeroes
that see past all excuse.
I move then
without sleep,

through each glass,
each blown tissue
and cheap affair. Blue body!
humming with phallic plastic
I never bargained for—I
who once was heavy,
spat acid and broke
what I touched.

Crystal Meth

The day comes on—the light crackling
through plastic-wrapped windows in the kitchen
or just out the door, hard

and hardly natural, a humming florescence
tunneling around you from this farm
              over to that: the rusted pump shrieking,

ice cakes that fog and hollow
in the fallow fields, acres of dead alfalfa stuck
in blank, factual March. Turn around,

sleepwalker, look. Those are the years
you stamped out with white-cross, those that you smothered
with a fuel-soaked rag. Your hatred for this place only simplifies
the delicate, dedicated work, a life
like a bone you've carved into lace

into this—long nights repeating
by the radio, the light bulb
the bales of bright straw.

Rotten May Pole

Hot clouds, the light pulsing
before the downpour and what

fantastic light! — churned avocado,
nervous milkmint, a dead swimming-pool's blue.

A fine drizzle, funny-scented
as tar, as old tin, begins.

Something will happen: the moon goes out,
flooded piss-green lawns expire

in mud. We're both mashed up on gin.
Sober, we tear at each other

clammy-skinned, exhausted
from sleep. We're tired

of this drudging,
this fruit-crushing dance.

Iphigeneia

She was so clean after we scrubbed her
and brushed her teeth
and made her small.
We put her in a martini to keep her
from growing old. And she never did
but grew dull, appalled,
her eyes and genitals opened up
not to blink.

Before They Found Mrs. McFarland in Her Car

Humid afternoons when nothing moved,
the sky gray, rainless—my brother and I crept

into the yard and garden
she'd let go, the apple tree never pruned.

We parted the low, heavy branches,
entered that droning dome: yellow jackets drifting,

wiring the green room with their currents of need
or reason, with whatever drives a yellow jacket.

We didn't eat the fruit but thrilled
in darkness, the sticky grass and mashed apples

underfoot—all those nervous creatures
wild with a sweetening pulp.

The Beautiful Aunt

What were you then
to me? I was thirteen, a Catholic
who knew that touching you,
my father's brother's wife, would send me

reeling to Hell. In that rented beach-house
I turned, burning in the sheets.
But I watched as you came
to kiss me goodnight, your full body

under thin cotton. In twelve years
you'd come out of sleep
as well, startled and shivering
in wet covers, until they discovered

the secret — a splitting of skins
beneath your skin, a code
gone haywire — and prescribed
a burning that turned you frail,

bald and limp as a rag. Aunt Dolly,
I see you now, as if for the first time:
a hesitant bride in the flash photo, smiling,
a little frightened in your white gown.

The Man who Sold the World

Say that every age demands it—someone to clear his throat
while we listen and turn, suddenly horrified but not surprised
by this: the old, ever-new rock star suicide—part minstrel
part comedian—tap-dancing away from us into his dark,
reducing all formalities to formula—what a show!
Showing up authority, sham the limits! Given, he has to be,
to giving up, a kind of disappearing act. The man who stands in
for finality—the blacked-up cocky *No*.

Me and Old Robert McGee
—for Joe Wenderoth

I am driving through town
past the redbuds, open finally
in filthy East Baltimore.
The sun, when it bothers to show up,
even late, as now, floods, doesn't it
swaddle us each, this girlish afternoon light?
And just as from my radio Janis Joplin
screams herself hoarse about feeling good
being good enough—gooseflesh rising at the thought
of everything having to end—now
an elderly gentleman, clearly retired,
spittle stringing from his chin, gets up
from his lawn chair to give me the finger.

The green glass
dust between and all around us
is also too brilliant,
too excruciating to overlook.

Southern Gothic (Abridged)

she did it   poor thing
oh he beat his children   once

before he shot himself   awful
unshaven and drunk in church

pregnant   gone
California maybe   a prostitute

don't know his own daughter sleeps with
women   I wouldn't sell your home

to no foreigner   no slick and tricky
stranger   I tell you what

you get what
                    you deserve

Letter to Tu Fu

In the end you wandered alone each spring, far
and farther from wife and child. And here it's April.
We're reading you through translation. No petals flying now.
This is our month of mud—
newspapers blown into the yard
and stuck, winter lingering in the unpaid bills.
Here spring's an idea without shape
our own children still abstractions, small
unbroken seeds far beneath us
a darkness under our words.

Lush Life

Staggering home each night
after closing-time, collapsing
onto the bed, the sofa, and one time
even the bathtub, poor broken
record, you.

What were you looking for?
That's easy—love, but the only thing
you remember now was the last Friday morning
of winter months, going out for coffee, the hangover
still ringing your skull and seeing on either side
of Saint Paul St.: evictions!
By their own cheap sofas, gold shoes
and negligee, spilled boxes of glass
jewelry in the gutter—the Call-Girls,
transvestites, tall and elegant still
but without their wigs, in ratty bathrobes
out without time to put on makeup, suddenly
forced to wander the streets in broken pumps—a few
in slippers—breasting the cold bright
morning, all of them, moving on
chin-high and stiff-lipped. And you, dumb
and open-mouthed: how

did they ever make it?
You never knew. Those people
suffered and survived
or died in other galaxies. But you
lived alone, small and terrified
of shadows and of yourself when each night
the evening in you tipped
his dark hat and grinned.

Pan American

You want to sit at the feet
        of the farmers you come from

who rose and dressed in the dark
        to work the earth again with raw fists,

who buried their children near and returned
        each evening hefting roots or potatoes

down to the cellar. You want to go back
        and live with those people

whom nothing could stop—not the floods, the barn-rot,
        not the snow-frozen livestock.

To be like them, you'd break your teeth,
        your bones, to build up a single, solid home.

You'd plow the fields by the whole day's light,
        driven by nothing but love.

But think how quiet they must be,
        the ones who earned their dirt

and wore out their skin,
        who plucked wooden instruments

on hand-hewn porches. Look at them grinning,
        their bones baked by sunset.

Look hard as you pass
        and look away. Let them be.

Crossing Minnesota at Night

Moon corn
beneath white planets

the barns
humming in milk-blue light.

Waiting for the Firstborn

   There you are! little egg, you—
dark and clinging to my wife's uterus which,
on the black and white monitor screen

right now, could easily be the ghostly ground-surface
people must have seen on their TVs of the first
lunar landing, almost before your dad's time.
He was crying, probably, hungry and still
getting used to the crib—the sixties closing up,
King and both Kennedys erased, so much darkness
and war on the planet, though it must have looked clean
from the moon and marble-y blue, set as it is
against the greater darkness of space.

The People—hardly quiet or united—did briefly that July
sit still to watch the astronauts in their white suits
bouncing over the powder slow and stiff
as cartoon figures, clicking photographs with time
enough to plant the flag, ham for the camera
or take a call from Nixon, the Commander
in Chief, before calling it a day. Then, climbing back up
into the Landing Module, they slept and awoke,
finally ready to blast off that lifeless rock

and twirl weightless again in space.
Back in Houston the longhaired reporters
and NASA crew-cuts who stayed up smoking
through cups and cups of coffee had never stopped,
on the other hand, sweating. Waiting for signs, voices
from spacecraft Apollo to come crackling back
through their radios, worrying over the numbers—
all that calculus—equations on a blackboard, endless variables
in each direction, the asymptotes, odds, and formulas.

Three days later the People returned, many of them
at least, to their television sets, though unlike the scientists,
with little physics and virtually no significant data, couples
on their new sofas praying, waiting through the tiny capsule's
long journey home. But more than anything, I can imagine
at this moment each astronaut's family sitting rigid before the screen,
swallowing, quietly mouthing or moaning that funny chant
that is really the world's oldest song.   *Hang on...*
Hang on, you son of a gun.   Come home.

Immigrant

Pick up, you say to yourself. It's your father
who provoked on account of his broken dialect
so much reserve and suspicion

the old voice across the long distance
gentle, no less compelling
the accent lingering. Even this late

he calls—and likes to—the same way
he still kisses you, still offers the finest cuts
of meat in the dream.

Notes

"Año Nuevo, 1992":
    "Bolívares" are Venezuelan units of currency named after Simón Bolívar.

"Watching Late-Night Hitchcock":
    The last line of Section 7. is similar to the phrase Robert Fitzgerald uses in his Introduction to Flannery O'Connor's *Everything that Rises Must Converge* (New York: Farrar, Straus and Giroux, 1999).

    Rilke's lines in Section 12. come from "The First Elegy" in his *Duino Elegies*. See *The Selected Poetry of Rainer Maria Rilke*, edited and translated by Stephen Mitchell, Vintage Inernational, 1989.

    The italicized portion of Section 13. comes from a marginal note Ezra Pound made on T.S. Eliot's manuscript of *The Waste Land*. See *T.S. Eliot The Waste Land: A Facsimile and Transcript of the Original Drafts Including the Annotations of Ezra Pound*, edited by Valerie Eliot, Harcourt Brace & Company, 1971.

"Fathers and Sons":
    "Led Zeppelin III," the third record by the rock band Led Zeppelin, opens with a track entitled "Immigrant Song."

"Pan American":
    This is also name of the Louisville and Nashville Railroad passenger train that initially linked Cincinnati to New Orleans. In existence from 1921 until 1971, this famous train inspired Hank Williams Sr.'s song of the same title.

Biographical Note

Peter Ramos grew up near Baltimore, Maryland. His poems appear in *Indiana Review*, *Painted Bride Quarterly*, *Poet Lore*, *The Chattahoochee Review*, *Fugue*, *Verse*, *MIPOesias*, and other journals. In 2000, his poem "Evolution" was nominated by *Meridian* for a Pushcart Prize.

He holds graduate degrees from George Mason University and the State University of New York at Buffalo. An Assistant Professor of English at Buffalo State College, Peter lives with his wife, Diane, in Buffalo, NY.

May 2008

Fernando —
It's wonderful to meet you and hear your beautiful poems.

Mucho Gusto!

ramospj@buffalostate.edu